ANIMAL TALK

What Do They Have To Say?

DEBRA SAUM

Copyright © 2012 Debra Saum
All rights reserved.

ISBN: 1470045494
ISBN-13: 9781470045494

ANIMAL TALK

What Do They Have To Say?

DEBRA SAUM

Introduction

If there's anything I've learned from the many years I've been talking to animals and painting their portraits, it's that they have so much to say. Sometimes they surprise me with their amazing wisdom and sometimes their humor makes me laugh out loud.

Their messages are always filled with wonder, an honest understanding about their lives and a strong desire to reach out to those humans who will listen to them. Whether they're speaking to children or conversing with adults, their hope is always the same:

They want us to hear them.

Animal Talk is a collection of my favorite animal portraits and the wonderful ideas these special characters have for all of us. I believe their portraits will speak directly to you and their words will fill your heart with joy.

"Let's Play"
Lion Club

"Heart of the Leo"
African Lion

"I am the symbol of wildness and
strength that lives in everything.
Embrace your own wildness and
you'll chase away fear.
Then you realize you're just like me and I'm
just like you....

**We're all
the same species.
The species called LIFE."**

"Being able to play all the time is what life's all about! People tell me to sit. What's the point? It's much more fun to run around and chase things. Lighten up!....

When you believe in mischief anything's possible!"

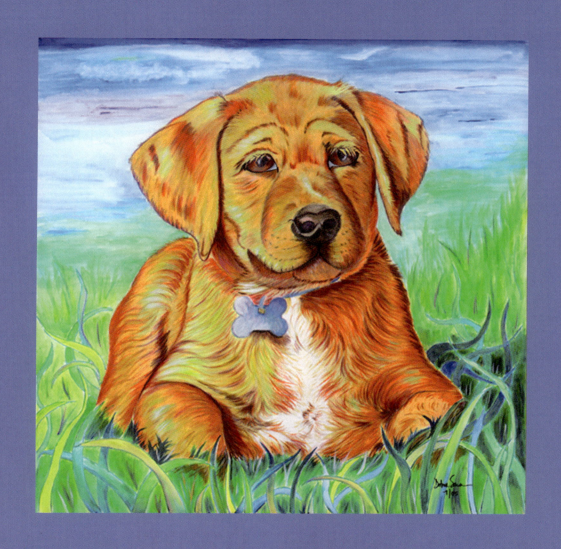

"Pure Mischief"
Mixed Breed Puppy

"Majani"

Cheetah Ambassador for Endangered Species

"People think I'm special. I'm just doing my job. I think it's important to be true to yourself and do the things you believe are good...

Life is more simple that way."

"I like to be around humans who say what they mean and mean what they say. The answers to life are simple:

Speak the truth
Stand up for what you believe
Act from your heart
Don't over-think everything."

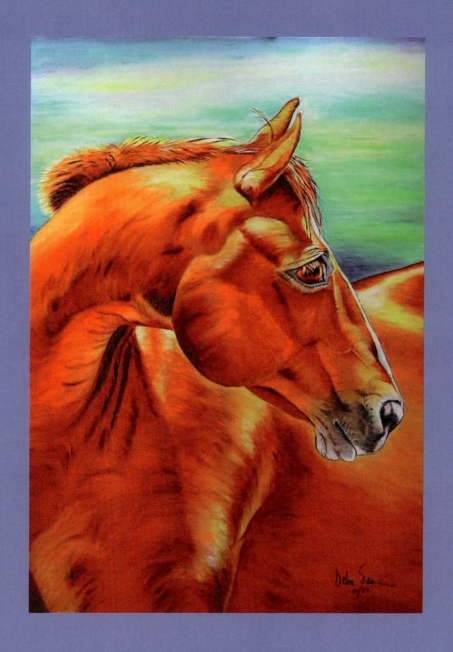

"ROMEO"
American Quarter Horse

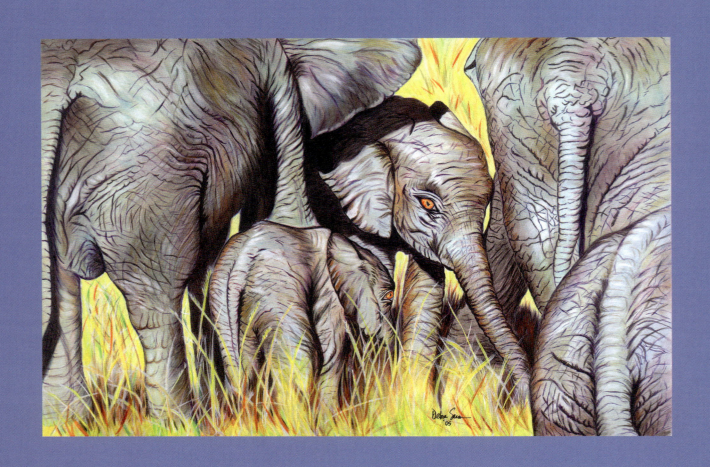

"REAR VIEW"
African Elephants

"Life is a series of endings……
and beginnings. The rear view
helps you remember where you
came from, so
you can look forward
to where you're going.

**Embrace your life,
it all counts."**

"Joy is everything. I live for joy! I'm handsome and powerful.....but the most important thing to me is being around people who are joyful and happy....

Spread your joy around!"

"PERUVIAN PRINCE"
Peruvian Paso Gelding

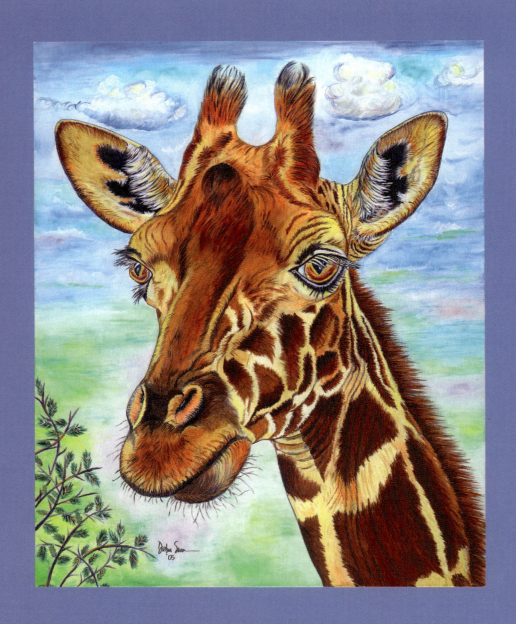

"HEAD IN THE CLOUDS"
African Giraffe

"It's a good idea to have your
head in the clouds....that's how
you stay in touch with thinking good thoughts.

**Real strength is in letting go
and being a cloud. Try it!"**

"I like chips and soda…….a lot. I've lived a long time and I've figured out what's important….it's whatever is happening right now. And I'd like some more chips. Right now.

Stuff only matters if you can eat it, smell it, or enjoy it."

"CHEETA"

Hollywood Companion of Tarzan

"LIVING THE DREAM"
American Quarter Horse

"It's easy to dream about what you want.
Believing in your dream is the key to living it.
Why not start now? It's not as hard as you think....

Just start believing."

"Sometimes you have to look right at something in order to understand it….. Sometimes not. Learn to look at things from a completely different point of view….

You'll be surprised how life gives you exactly what you want."

"HERE'S LOOKING AT YOU"
African Leopard

"KILLI'S EYES"
Domestic Short-haired Tabby

"Love is all there is. When I open my eyes wide and purr, people love on me. Joy and Love….they're the same thing.

**Let somebody love on you.
You'll experience joy."**

"Honesty is everything.
When you speak from your heart,
you're telling the truth....

Listen to your heart.
It never lies."

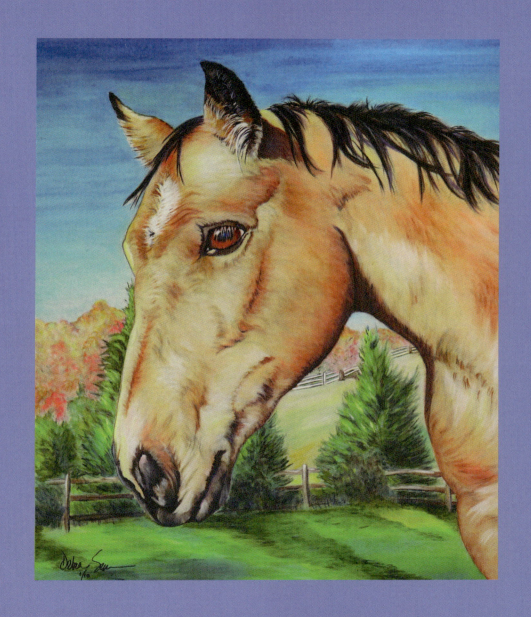

"KILARNEY"
Buckskin Mare

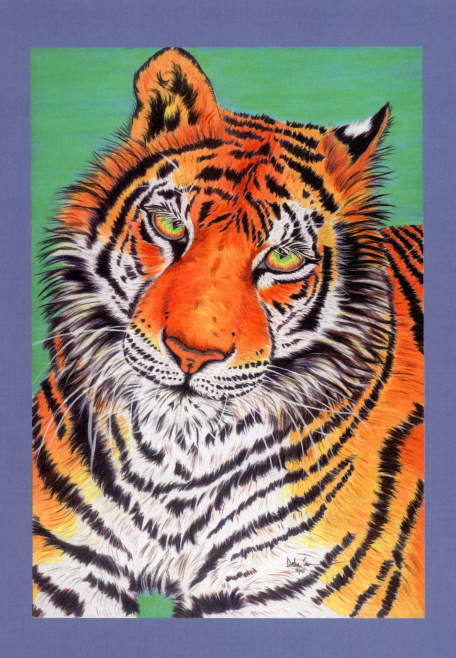

"NOBLE MESSENGER"
Siberian Tiger

"Power is an energy that lives inside you. It comes alive when you peacefully listen to your own inner beauty. You can find your true self with that power....

You can save the world with that power."

"Being a leader is just as important as being a follower. Harmony and happiness occur when everyone embraces their place in the herd. Life is like that too.....

When you find your place, you find your strength."

"HERD LEADER"
African Zebra

"SLEW BOY'S TENT"
Thoroughbred Gelding

"Curiosity is a healthy habit. As soon as you think you know something, curiosity nudges you to look again. If you want to live a long and happy life,

Invite curiosity to dance with you whenever possible."

"People say 'It's a jungle out there'.
What a great idea! Happiness is my jungle....
maybe your jungle can be <u>your</u> happiness.

**It all depends on
how you look at it."**

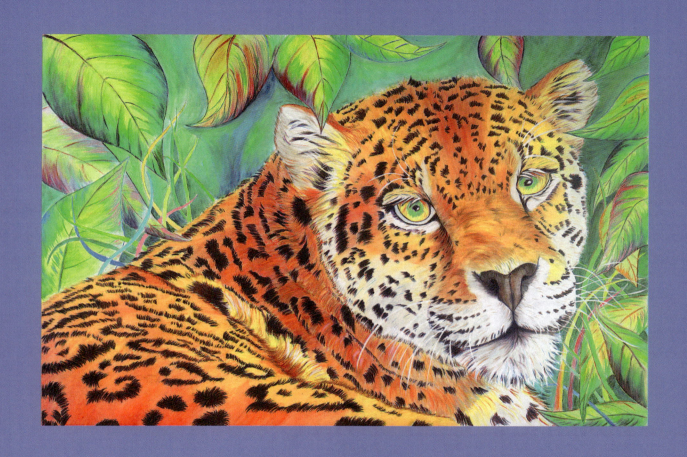

"HAPPINESS IS A JUNGLE"
Jaguar

"WALK YOUR TALK"
African Elephants

"Being true to yourself gives you
the courage to believe in who you are,
the strength to always be fair,
and the ability to feel joyful all the time.

**Trust in the soul of kindness…
it is your most precious resource."**

Made in the USA
Lexington, KY
29 September 2012